T0119404

Be more Jane

Be more Jane

BRING OUT YOUR INNER AUSTEN
TO MEET LIFE'S CHALLENGES

SOPHIE ANDREWS

Illustrated by Jane Odiwe

CICO BOOKS

LONDON NEW YORK

Published in 2019 by CICO Books
An imprint of Ryland Peters & Small Ltd
20–21 Jockey's Fields   341 E 116th St
London WC1R 4BW   New York, NY 10029

www.rylandpeters.com

10 9 8 7 6 5 4 3 2 1

Text © Sophie Andrews 2019
Design and illustration © CICO Books 2019

A CIP catalog record for this book is available from the
Library of Congress and the British Library.

ISBN: 978 1 78249 706 6

Printed in China

Designer: Geoff Borin
Illustrator: Jane Odiwe

Art director: Sally Powell
Head of production: Patricia Harrington
Publishing manager: Penny Craig
Publisher: Cindy Richards

Contents

Introduction

When I was at the tender age of nine, on one rainy afternoon in Berkshire, my mother sat me down to watch a new movie: the 2005 film adaptation of *Pride and Prejudice*. Little did either of us realize then how significant Jane Austen was to become in my life. A few years later, my school English teacher encouraged me to read Austen's novels, and immediately I was caught up in the elegance and eloquence of her world and words; since then, I have devoted myself to all aspects of the astonishing Jane Austen phenomenon. Aged sixteen, I began my blog, "Laughing with Lizzie," and to my great surprise, it quickly became popular, so I am now privileged to have thousands of followers across various social media platforms and to have made many wonderful new friends, all of whom share my passion for all things Austen.

In 2015, it was an honor to become an ambassador for the wonderful charity The Jane Austen Literacy Foundation, founded by Jane Austen's fifth-great niece, Caroline Jane Knight. In the same year I founded the Jane Austen Pineapple Appreciation Society (JAPAS) and began organizing social events such as picnics, balls, festival visits, and house parties for my Janeite friends, all in full Regency dress. The year 2017 was unique and significant, as we marked the bicentenary of Jane Austen's death. From starring in the BBC TV documentary "My Friend Jane," to featuring in the UK's *Guardian* newspaper, I was privileged to be involved in so many of the celebrations.

Jane Austen has always been my escape. Her novels and letters have brought laughter, her characters have become familiar friends, and I have learned crucial lessons on coping with life's trials and tribulations. Perhaps through my book you will also enjoy being reminded of some of Austen's words of wisdom. They have certainly spoken to me, and I feel they are still as relevant today as they were in Austen's own era. I do hope Miss Austen wouldn't mind that I have also had some fun exploring the—often amusing—attitudes of some of my favorite personalities from her novels and have been inspired to create a few character vignettes.

I am so very grateful to my dear and talented friend Jane Odiwe for the beautiful and colorful illustrations that enhance my text so perfectly and bring Austen's Regency world to life.

So now, I hope you will enjoy dipping into the observations of Jane Austen and that you too will learn to "be more Jane"!

Be More Lizzy

"I dearly love a laugh."

(Pride and Prejudice)

Elizabeth "Lizzy" Bennet is one of the most well known, admired, and popular of Jane Austen's heroines. Witty, independent, intelligent, loyal, and a loving daughter and sister, she is perhaps the character most closely linked in the reader's mind to Jane Austen herself. Since my first introduction to Lizzy, when I was just 16, she has been my inspiration. She has been my blog persona for a number of years and, from her, I have picked up invaluable tips on how to be more of a "Lizzy" in my own life.

Life can be tough, so try to make it fun and enjoyable more of the time. Lizzy herself declares, "follies and nonsense, whims and inconsistencies do divert me, I own, and I laugh at them whenever I can" and we should do the same. Lizzy always searches for the funny side to any situation, which is a sensible approach to life, for laughing is proven to be good for us. In today's challenging world, where we are faced with negativity on a daily basis, it is essential to find joy in as much as we can, to keep us smiling.

"You have widely mistaken my character, if you think I can be worked on by such persuasions as these."

These are Lizzy's defiant words during her clash with Lady Catherine de Bourgh, after rumors reach her ladyship of an engagement between Lizzy and her nephew, Mr Darcy. Elizabeth is a wonderful example of someone who knows her own mind and will not be persuaded to do anything she does not believe in. She is even strong enough to stand up to Lady Catherine, a formidable character, of far superior rank in society—no mean feat! Lizzy is someone who will always fight her own corner but is not afraid to support others when needed. She shows real courage and commendable strength of character, particularly for a woman in the Regency era. We can follow in her footsteps, be true to what we know is right, and stand up for our beliefs.

These are the two principal lessons to be learned from our inspirational heroine, and they are two that have particularly helped me.

But it also seems to me that occasionally walking through a muddy field, as Lizzy famously does, might not be such a bad idea when seeking to impress! And perhaps she knows a trick or two when, out of curiosity, she unexpectedly goes visiting a rich man's house and estate and successfully wins his love (and his fortune!).

BE MORE LIZZY

Seek out the fun in life.

Stand up for what you believe in.

Don't worry about getting a bit of mud on your shoes!

Jane on Love

> "I suppose there may be a hundred different
> ways of being in love."
>
> *(Emma)*

At their core, each of Austen's six main novels has love as the central theme and concludes with the happy ending we all desire for our heroines, yet the stories differ hugely in the way each love story develops. The portraits Jane Austen paints of the many facets of love are realistic and still recognizable to us today. When compared with the melodramatic Gothic romances which were a prevalent and popular genre at the time (and which she parodied in *Northanger Abbey*), her approach was original and groundbreaking.

Arguably the most well-known love story is that of Elizabeth Bennet and Mr Darcy in *Pride and Prejudice*. In fact, their hate-turns-to-love relationship has inspired other authors and also screenwriters and has become the foundation of many a love story and rom-com since, from Mrs Gaskell's *North and South* to the Austen-inspired *Bridget Jones's Diary*.

Sense and Sensibility highlights the slow development of true love, with both Elinor and Marianne having to go through sadness before finding their happy ending. Elinor has to wait for the misguided Edward Ferrars to disentangle himself from his secret engagement to Lucy Steele, which he regrets heavily but is too honorable to rescind, while Marianne suffers a very public humiliation by Willoughby, before realizing the true worth of Colonel Brandon, and her love for him.

Emma Woodhouse and Mr Knightley in *Emma*, and Fanny Price and Edmund Bertram in *Mansfield Park*, are both examples of long-term friendships turning, in time, to love. And in *Persuasion*, Anne Elliot and Captain Wentworth show us that second chances are possible, even if you think all "hope is gone"!

"What a strange thing love is!"

So says Emma Woodhouse. For a short while, Emma imagines herself to be enamored with the recently returned Mr Frank Churchill, but later realizes she was only flattered by his attentions and had been swept along by the hopes and wishes of Churchill's father, Mr Weston. Harriet Smith is persuaded to think herself smitten with a succession of eligible bachelors, before realizing her first was the genuine emotion:

> "and it was too much to hope even of Harriet, that she could be in love with more than three men in one year."

We all have our own love stories, some of which are still waiting to be written, but each of them is individual and personal, even if it bears similarities to others.

LEARN FROM JANE

Don't confuse love with infatuation.

There is no right or wrong way to fall in love.

Not every love story begins with a misunderstanding.

MRS BENNET'S GUIDE
TO SUCCESSFUL ENGAGEMENTS

My dear Mr Bennet and I were not blessed with a son and heir, but with five daughters, thus my constant concern is that our estate is abominably entailed away to an odious distant cousin. I cannot begin to tell you what this does to my poor nerves! So with this future predicament looming over me, you will understand that I have had to become adept in the art of putting my daughters in the way of eligible bachelors, in order to facilitate marriage proposals. I believe that by following my advice, you too might secure the best possible future for your own daughters, and— through them—for yourself in your later years.

• You must be sure to remain fully involved in local society, thereby to be among the first to hear of any new single man who is come into your neighborhood. Most importantly, you should without delay ascertain his position in society and his eligibility, as well as his precise income, the whereabouts of his estate, and the number of carriages he owns.

• Require of your husband that he be quick to introduce himself to the newcomer as soon as ever he can—you will desire that this take place before other local gentlemen with daughters do likewise. I am reminded here that on one occasion, I feared that my husband, Mr Bennet, was not intending to visit a newly arrived and particularly wealthy bachelor, Mr Bingley of Netherfield, but then it transpired he was only teasing me—he takes such delight in vexing me and has no compassion on my poor nerves! My reliable husband did indeed visit the charming Mr Bingley, with five thousand a year, and my aspirations of attracting Mr Bingley's attentions toward my eldest and prettiest daughter, Jane, were soon fulfilled.

• Once introduced, and at the earliest opportunity, be sure to have the eligible new acquaintance dance with your daughter at a ball, be it public or private. If you can secure the first two dances of the evening for her, so much the better! (Just think of the significant message that will send to your neighbors, when they observe your daughter as a favorite and a preferred dance partner!) The better way to secure your daughter as his choice for the dances, I think, is to position yourself correctly in the ballroom. This will allow you to be first to greet him on his arrival at the ball and make the required introductions. Do not be shy to point out your daughter's fine looks and excellent virtues—a little exaggeration works wonders if needed, especially if you are not blessed with the most handsome or talented daughter. (It has been such a trial to find a suitable husband for my poor dear Mary…) You must make him feel obligated to ask your daughter to dance first, since she is above all others in her looks and manner, and indeed, it would be very rude of him if he did not!

• The next step might well be an invitation to call at the home of your chosen suitor and his family. And here is a trick! Find reason that your daughter may not travel by carriage but must go on horseback, and then if the weather should take a turn to rain, she will have cause to stay longer, even for the night! Is this not a very good scheme of mine? For it worked very well for my dear Jane, who most fortuitously caught a chill on her way to take tea with Mr Bingley's sister, such that she must trespass on the Bingleys' hospitality not just for one night, but for several, and I could not have been happier!

Most importantly, you should without delay ascertain his position in society and his eligibility, as well as his precise income, the whereabouts of his estate, and the number of carriages he owns.

• If an opportunity arises, it would be a good plan to encourage your daughter's potential suitor to host a ball in her honor—the other guests will soon discern any developing attachment, and with some encouragement, a proposal must be forthcoming. Meanwhile, you might in all humility be permitted to drop a few hints of an imminent engagement

into your conversations, in order to discourage interference from other interested parties.

If you pursue these objectives, I feel certain you will have your daughters all well settled in no time.

• If, like me, you are faced with the affliction of having your family home entailed elsewhere, it would be wise to facilitate a match between the heir to your estate and one of your daughters. This also had been an intention of mine; however, it is in this instance alone that my scheming went awry. The heir chose to make a proposal to the most stubborn and headstrong of our five daughters, Elizabeth, and that silly girl was so thoughtless as to refuse him. She remained obstinate, despite my threat that I would never see her again; I would have continued to insist, had not my husband sided with Elizabeth for some unreasonable and unfathomable purpose. I am sure, however, that you will have more success in this endeavor than I, provided you are blessed with a more sensible and supportive husband.

(Although I will say, I have since forgiven my Lizzy, for she managed to secure for herself one of the richest and most eligible bachelors in the whole of England, Mr Darcy of Pemberley in Derbyshire, a most arrogant and unpleasant man to my way of thinking, yet his ten thousand a year will guarantee her a life of luxury and comfort, which will make up for it I am sure.)

If you pursue these objectives, I feel certain you will have your daughters all well settled in no time.

Jane on Patience

"Do not be in a hurry, the right man will come at last."

(Letter)

This invaluable piece of advice appears in a letter from Jane Austen to her young niece, Fanny Knight.

We probably all have friends, neighbors, or even family members who have been in a bad relationship or have married someone who turns out to be the wrong one for them. Or perhaps a friend has confided their fears of getting "too old," imagining that their chance of finding a life partner has passed them by.

Jane Austen reminds us of the need to wait and to commit ourselves wisely; she encourages the reader through her portrayal of characters whose patience is rewarded, while cautioning us with examples of unhappy marriages made in haste.

When talking to Janeites, I have found it fascinating to discover how many initially thought *Pride and Prejudice* to be their favorite novel, until later they were drawn more to *Persuasion*, perhaps because their life experiences had brought greater understanding, and an appreciation of second chances, hope, and patience. Anne Elliot waits for over eight years for a second chance with Wentworth, the "right man" for her. Having been persuaded to reject a proposal from him when she was younger, Anne is now 27 and considered an old maid by Regency standards! Both Anne and Wentworth have remained faithful to their hope of a future together, and when they meet again, they rediscover their love. Finally, Anne wins her naval captain. Not, however, without first suffering considerable nervous apprehension and a few misunderstandings.

While Austen's letter recommends her niece await "the right man," in her novels, we frequently meet a gentleman having to wait for his right woman too. In *Emma*, Mr Knightley must watch from the sidelines and conceal his feelings while he waits for Emma Woodhouse to mature, until she finally comes to recognize her love for him. Poor Robert Martin, in the same novel, endures a long wait for Harriet Smith thanks to

Emma's interference. And in *Sense and Sensibility*, Colonel Brandon's constancy is finally rewarded when Marianne Dashwood comes to realize he is her soulmate, setting aside her infatuation with the handsome and exciting but weak-willed fortune seeker, Mr Willoughby—although it does take a serious illness to bring her to her senses!

We know that Jane Austen herself initially accepted an offer of marriage, but then quickly changed her mind and turned down the offer, perhaps knowing she would not be truly happy and should continue to be patient. This was a very bold decision, for at that time a suitable marriage would have been of the utmost importance to a lady in her situation, and indeed society would have considered it a necessity. It is possible that Jane Austen preferred to be single, so that she could continue to write; however, it is an ironic but sad truth that although Jane writes happy endings for all her heroines, she herself never found the right man.

BELIEVE IN JANE

Trust that patience will pay off, however doubtful it might seem at times.

Stay positive and hopeful—it is never too late to find the one for you.

The right one is worth waiting for—although hopefully not for eight years, like Anne Elliot!

Jane on Appearances

> "One has got all the goodness, and the other all the appearance of it."

(Pride and Prejudice)

So says Lizzy to her sister Jane toward the conclusion of *Pride and Prejudice*, as they compare Mr Darcy's integrity and kindness to the seemingly handsome and debonair Mr Wickham's web of lies.

The original title of *Pride and Prejudice* was *First Impressions*, reflecting the importance and influence they have in the story. It is a significant lesson that, however good a judge of character we think we may be, first impressions can be misleading, and we can certainly be mistaken about people.

It's not just Lizzy who is taken in and later sees the light. In *Emma*, Emma Woodhouse is ignorant at first of Mr Elton's true nature and intentions, thinking him a perfect match for her friend Harriet, when he is, in fact, hoping to marry Emma herself. In *Sense and Sensibility*, Willoughby is an accomplished charmer, who manages to keep his shameful past a secret, until Marianne has been deceived and discarded. But of course the most obvious example is Lizzy condemning Mr Darcy after their first meeting, and yet being so trusting of the deceitful Mr Wickham! (Although Mr Darcy really did nothing to help himself on the evening of their first acquaintance—no one wants to be described as "tolerable"!)

When making new friends, or meeting colleagues for the first time, we should allow ourselves time to get to know each other.

LEARN FROM LIZZY

First impressions cannot always be trusted.

Some people tell a good story… but it takes time to establish the truth.

Do not be taken in by a handsome young man in uniform!

Jane on Self-Belief

> "Laugh as much as you choose, but you will not laugh me out of my opinion."

(Pride and Prejudice)

Lizzy Bennet has been hearing tales from Mr Wickham of Darcy treating him poorly and ruining his career. When she relates them to her sister, Jane is at pains to remind Lizzy to be fair-minded and to be sure of all the facts before condemning Mr Darcy. Even Jane, the quieter of the two sisters, trusts her own judgment.

Lizzy, and Marianne Dashwood in *Sense and Sensibility*, are both confident heroines who are not afraid to speak their mind and be their own person, although with varying results. Austen uses other characters to show that pretending to be someone you are not rarely has a good outcome. In *Emma*, as Harriet Smith increasingly receives firm guidance from Emma Woodhouse, she starts to imitate Emma, her social superior, which only results in confusion and unhappiness. In *Pride and Prejudice*, Kitty Bennet seems under the influence of her younger sister, Lydia, as she tries to copy her fun-loving but arguably selfish approach to life.

Two of our heroes, Mr Knightley in *Emma* and Mr Tilney in *Northanger Abbey*, are self-assured and confident. They do not change, but are presented from the start as models of sensible, straight-talking, good people. They provide a strong contrast to their heroine counterparts— Emma and Catherine Morland both mature and learn from their mistakes, until they each experience moments of enlightenment and recognition of their own feelings. We are all different and you *can* be your own person.

LEARN FROM JANE

From self-belief come confidence and courage.

Don't imitate others, however much you admire them.

Be proud of who you are, and an "obstinate, headstrong girl" if necessary!

WHAT TO AVOID WHEN TRYING
TO ATTRACT A GENTLEMAN

by Marianne Dashwood and Louisa Musgrove

We have each experienced trials and tribulations in the pursuit of a young man, often caused by our own poor decisions. We have come together to admit to our mistakes, so that you might avoid making such errors of judgement yourselves.

Marianne

I begin with lessons I have learned on my journey to find love.

• Stay inside when it is wet; do not be tempted to think it romantic to go out in the rain. I had two unfortunate incidents in inclement weather. On the first occasion, I slipped and fell, spraining my ankle, and although I was rescued by a charming and handsome young man, Mr John Willoughby, he turned out to be a devious and faithless scoundrel. The second circumstance was a walk in heavy rain, causing me to catch a serious chill! This latter incident did bring me to my senses, helping me recognize the admirable qualities of my future husband, Colonel Brandon; nevertheless I do not recommend you follow my example by ignoring the weather. Stay safely indoors, and admire the elements from a warm and dry location, thus avoiding any risk of illness or injury.

• Be wary of young men who pretend to all the same tastes and opinions as you. If, like me, you are a romantic creature with a love of poetry, or you "have a passion for dead leaves" (as my sister once observed in jest), be careful of a man who claims to enjoy and appreciate all the same things as you. There is a strong possibility that it is all pretence, in order to impress and please you. I was once taken in by such flattery. Moreover, I have learned that differences in opinion and interests are preferable, as they make for interesting discussion and create opportunities to learn.

• Reflect on your behavior, and how it will be perceived by other people. While I strongly believe in expressing myself freely in words and deeds, my ordeal with the reprehensible Mr Willoughby taught me to conduct myself with more decorum, and to consider the impression one makes. I have come to the realization that I caused upset, confusion, and uncertainty through my thoughtless conduct, especially to my own family. So be careful not to flirt shamelessly and blatantly, particularly when in company, nor should you ever be alone with a young man without a chaperone.

• Avoid writing revealing letters to a man—particularly in the middle of the night or very early in the morning—until you are betrothed. And even if he should ask nicely, do not bestow on a man a meaningful token such as a lock of your hair, unless the recipient is your intended.

• Age does not signify where true love is concerned. This has been perhaps my most important lesson, for I once thought my dear Brandon too old for me. But when I finally realized his irrefutable integrity, his gentle and caring nature, and our shared appreciation of music, my love for him grew deeper. Age is not important; in fact, I now believe older gentlemen may even make more loving and dependable partners in life.

Reflect on your behavior, and how it will be perceived by other people.

Louisa

I too have had some regrettable experiences along the path to a happy marriage. I believe I have two important pieces of advice to add.

• Look before you leap—literally!

Do not jump off things, however big or small. I once thought it amusing, and an excellent way to seek attention, to jump off gates during a country walk, or down the stairs, or off a sea wall. There is always a hope that the gentleman you are eager to attract will catch you in his arms—or so I thought. It seemed such a lark until the day when, in my exuberance, I jumped from too great a height and could not be caught! I suffered a bad head injury, causing my poor family serious concern. It was a most reckless and thoughtless action and I have not jumped from high places since.

• Allow that love can develop when you least expect it.

While my injury was severe, it led to my betrothal to Captain Benwick, a man I mistakenly thought I could never love, as he seemed to me so dull and melancholy at first. But during my long recuperation, I came to realize the depth of his character and to appreciate his kind attentions. We formed a sincere attachment and are now blessed with a happy marriage. He has even helped me discover a love for poetry!

We both hope that you will heed our advice and that you manage to avoid the follies and dangerous situations we have described, when on your own path to finding true love and happiness.

Jane on Jealousy

> "Her jealousy and dislike of one sister much exceeded
> her affection for the other."

(Pride and Prejudice)

Jealousy is such a powerful emotion that it can destroy friendships and ruin lives. We will all have experienced moments of envy: as a child, there was probably a playmate who owned the toy we wanted; as an adult, we might covet a neighbor's new car, or resent a colleague's promotion at work, and of course sibling rivalry is also common. In Jane's novels, the emotion often portrayed is jealousy in love, and this causes nothing but unhappiness.

The quotation above refers to Caroline Bingley, who greatly resents her rival in love, Elizabeth Bennet. Caroline has so far failed to secure the proposal from Mr Darcy she hopes for, and when she begins to suspect Mr Darcy's interest in Lizzy, she becomes jealous. Caroline does her utmost to disparage Lizzy, with criticisms and fault-finding, and by maliciously teasing Darcy about the "charming mother-in-law" he would obtain if he married Lizzy! Of course, Darcy is not swayed. In fact Caroline's attempts even backfire on her: when Lizzy walks three muddy miles to visit her poorly sister, Caroline snidely remarks:

> "I am afraid, Mr. Darcy, that this adventure has rather
> affected your admiration of her fine eyes."

And the retort?

> "Not at all, they were brightened by the exercise."

Well, she tried!

Unfortunately for Caroline, her jealousy causes her nothing but bitterness and heartbreak. In desperation, and much later in the novel, she has a final attempt at changing Darcy's opinion of Lizzy. She criticizes all aspects of Lizzy's appearance, and her "self-sufficiency," and reminds Darcy that he himself did not initially find her pretty. His final retort, calling Lizzy "one of the handsomest women of my acquaintance" gives spiteful Caroline "no one any pain but [Caroline] herself."

The Bertram sisters in *Mansfield Park* are also affected by jealousy. Maria is promised to Mr Rushworth, a man she does not love, and quickly becomes jealous of her unattached sister, who receives all the attention from the handsome and eligible newcomer, Mr Crawford. Much then ensues in this love triangle, sisterly bonds are wrecked, and it all ends very badly indeed for Maria.

Even our heroine Emma Woodhouse, in *Emma*, struggles with feelings of resentment toward Jane Fairfax. She has heard Jane's virtues and accomplishments extolled so highly that she mistakenly sees her as a threat, and feels she needs to match or even surpass Jane in all things. Unfortunately, Emma never succeeds, and when the young ladies do eventually meet, she has a hard time liking poor Jane, for no justifiable reason.

Austen shows us that jealousy is a negative force, best avoided, and we would do well to overturn or resist such emotions.

DON'T BE LIKE CAROLINE

Don't allow resentments to ruin valued relationships.

Be the nicer you and celebrate the successes of your friends.

Never fish for compliments—you may not get the result that you were hoping for!

Jane on True Friends

"I do not want people to be very agreeable, as it saves
me the trouble of liking them a great deal."

(Letter)

Here, in one of her many letters to her sister Cassandra, is Jane Austen
at her most wry! Is she being quite particular here, even a bit cynical?
Or does it show how she values having a few true friends rather than
numerous acquaintances? It has been suggested that she did not enjoy
the social formalities required of her when she lived in Bath—visiting
acquaintances for tea, or mingling in society at the Pump Rooms.

People do drift in and out of our lives, at different stages—school
friends, college roommates, work colleagues, those we meet through
our hobbies and interests, or people who live in our neighborhood.
Our friendship circle changes as life progresses, but a few true friends
will stay with us throughout.

In *Pride and Prejudice*, the close friendship between Lizzy Bennet and
Charlotte Lucas is tested when Charlotte accepts a marriage proposal
from the laughable Mr Collins, whom Lizzy herself has recently rejected.
Charlotte specifically asks for her friend's understanding of their differing
attitudes to marriage:

"When you have had time to think it over, I hope you
will be satisfied with what I have done. I am not romantic,
you know; I never was."

Lizzy's initial shock and dismay at her friend's compromise turns to
acceptance and support and their friendship remains strong, even after
Charlotte marries and moves away.

In *Persuasion*, Anne Elliot is a staunch friend to her old schoolfellow
Mrs Smith, now an impoverished young widow struggling with ill health.
Anne visits and confides in her, despite the strong family disapproval
caused by differences in their social positions, and it is this friendship that
leads to the discovery of William Elliot's true nature and intentions.

Jane Austen was particularly close to two sisters, Catherine and Alethea Bigg. In fact, they were such good friends that their friendship survived Jane's initial acceptance, and then refusal, of the marriage proposal she received from their brother, Harris Bigg-Wither.

Cherish your close friends, however young you are, and if you are lucky, there will be some you keep for a long time. Despite Jane Austen's tongue-in-cheek assertion about saving herself the trouble of liking people, I look forward to crossing paths and making friends with many new and "very agreeable" people in times to come.

LEARN FROM JANE

Cherish your closest, most loyal friends, and show them loyalty in return.

Don't allow an unfortunate choice of partner to come between you and a true friend.

Some friendships will last, others will come and go—but that's life!

Jane on Marriage

"A woman is not to marry a man merely
because she is asked."

(Emma)

Wise words from the financially independent Miss Woodhouse, but unfortunately, this was often the most sensible course of action in Jane Austen's time. Love in marriage, though desirable, was a luxury. For many women, denied the opportunity to work or to inherit property, marriage was essential to gain financial security or better their social status.

Upper class women might have to accept a proposal from a man they barely knew and had never had a private conversation with, other than perhaps during a dance or two! Arranged marriages and marriages of convenience are still commonplace in some cultures today, but many of us are lucky enough to have the freedom to choose whom we marry, and to expect that love will come first.

When considering Jane Austen's six main novels, all but one of her heroines face the need to find a husband as soon as they can, in order to secure their own future and sometimes that of their relations too. Poor Mrs Bennet in *Pride and Prejudice* is mocked for excessive eagerness and lack of subtlety in her matchmaking, but the urgency to marry off her five daughters is more forgivable when you consider her constant fear of losing the family home to their cousin Mr Collins, Mr Bennet's entailed heir.

Austen also shows the unfortunate results of rushing into marriage. Mr and Mrs Bennet are two very different personalities and we are told that Mr Bennet,

"captivated by youth and beauty, and that appearance of
good humour which youth and beauty generally give,
had married a woman whose weak understanding and
illiberal mind had, very early in their marriage, put an end
to all real affection for her."

Lydia's eventual marriage to Wickham, under duress, seems doomed to follow the same path.

In *Mansfield Park*, Maria Bertram tumbles into a regrettable marriage with Mr Rushworth which ends in misery and scandal (and proves to be not "worth the rush" after all). Louisa Hurst, Mr Bingley's sister, also appears to be in a loveless marriage, relying heavily on the companionship of her sister, Caroline.

Charlotte Lucas may seem shockingly pragmatic to readers today, as she does to Lizzy, when she says, "happiness in marriage is entirely a matter of chance," but within the social restraints of the time she was right. Gaining financial security and not becoming an old maid, and thereby a burden on your parents or brothers, had to be the top priority. If you then grew to love your partner, that was a bonus.

Holding out for love was a risk, as Jane Austen herself discovered. She turned down a marriage proposal and remained unmarried until she died. Perhaps that is to our benefit, as it is likely that she would not have been able to write her wonderful novels if she were a wife and mother and running a home!

LEARN FROM JANE'S CHARACTERS

Be grateful if you are free to choose whether to marry or not.

Marry in haste, repent at leisure.

If you have made an unfortunate match, try to be in a different room to your spouse as much of the time as possible!

THE PERFECT WAY TO CATCH A HUSBAND!
—ACCORDING TO MISS LYDIA BENNET

Now that I am Mrs George Wickham, I am the happy wife of a handsome redcoat, no less! Moreover, as I am the first of five sisters to marry, even though I am the youngest, I clearly know the best ways of securing a husband. I am sure you will want to know how I did it. So I will share my ideas with you, then perhaps you too will have some of my good fortune!

• First, you must make sure you are noticed at every social occasion. Be noisy and lively and extrovert, and by all means, flirt most daringly at every opportunity! For if you are not coquettish, to indicate your obvious interest to young men, then how will you make one propose to you? While any handsome young gentleman of means would be acceptable, I suppose, I do believe (as does my dear mother) that to attract a smart officer in uniform is infinitely preferable. I have discovered that soldiers are all in need of pretty companions and are receptive to flirtatious behavior. I find they are so much more amusing than other gentlemen too, and always up for larks and frivolity and dancing. (Oh la! How I do laugh when I recall the time when we dressed up one of the officers to pass as a woman—what a good joke it was!) Oh yes, and I can reveal another good trick of mine to draw an officer's attention: steal something of theirs— even their sword!—and make them chase after you to get it back!

• Dance every dance! When you attend a ball, be sure to fill your card. It is boring to sit out for even a single dance. You must catch as many different partners as you can. (I have tried to explain this to my sister Mary, but she is such a dull creature and prefers her books and piano-playing to dancing and flirting. I do not think she shall ever marry!) If you are attending a private soirée or other such gathering, even if dancing is not supposed to happen, be sure to initiate a few sets. You must never pass up any opportunity! There is likely to be someone present who can play a jig on the pianoforte—it is so much more entertaining and enjoyable than listening to some boring old concerto or other.

• If, as I did, you have the prodigious good fortune to have a militia stationed in your locality, you must visit town just as often as you can find an excuse! If your papa does not approve, you must invent some good reason, like needing new ribbons for a ball or trimmings for a bonnet. The more you meet the officers, the more they will take a fancy to you. And here's yet another splendid plan of mine: visit their camp early in the day, and perhaps you will come upon them before they are dressed! What a shock they would get and how you would all laugh!

Elope if necessary.

• Brighton is the best place to get a husband. I was invited to summer with the officers in Brighton. (Just imagine my delight: a summer spent with a whole campful of soldiers! Not to mention the sea-bathing! La!) It was there that I procured my charming husband, Mr Wickham, so it must be the best place to go for husbands and all the better if you can catch a redcoat!

• Elope if necessary. If this is the opportunity that is presented to you, then take it! I find it safer to do exactly as your man wishes, for if you run away together, it means he intends to wed you, even if it does not take place immediately. Wickham and I had a stay in London before we married—it was so exciting! Some people may think elopement a scandal, but I never experienced any such thing, so I do not know what they mean. Just think what a pleasant surprise it will be to all your family, if you are unattached when you leave them and then write to them as a married lady! How they will laugh with joy, and how jealous your sisters will be!

I hope my own success and my advice above will encourage you to go and catch yourself a husband just as soon as may be, and hopefully even a redcoat, like mine. Though you will not find one as fine as my dear Mr Wickham, for there is none as perfect and as handsome as my darling husband!

Jane on Happiness

> "Think only of the past as its remembrance gives you pleasure."
>
> *(Pride and Prejudice)*

When Lizzy Bennet speaks these words to Mr Darcy, shortly after their engagement, she is asking Darcy to forget the previous misunderstandings and angry words spoken between them. The past cannot be changed, so live in the present and look to the future.

Even for the 19th century, Jane Austen died young at only 41, yet she had seen many highs and lows during her life and sometimes drew upon these personal experiences for her novels. Her early life was one of moderate wealth and comfort. However, when her father died, the family's standard of living and position in society slowly slipped lower, so that she ultimately became dependent on the goodwill of her brother.

Share Lizzy's philosophy. Life IS short. And it is full of ups and downs and unexpected turns. However, we can achieve so much if we live life to the full, and do not make excuses—listen to Frank Churchill in *Emma*:

> "How often is happiness destroyed by preparation, foolish preparation!"

Seize the day, and don't overthink things. We do best if we do not dwell on the past—on things that have happened, or should have happened, or could have happened—but live in the present and enjoy every day.

LEARN FROM LIZZY

Remember the good things that have happened in the past, and try not to dwell on the bad.

Avoid regrets—if you want to do something, don't delay.

You can't see around the next corner, so don't worry about what's waiting there for you.

Jane on the Role of Women

> "A woman, especially, if she have the misfortune of knowing anything, should conceal it as well as she can."
>
> *(Northanger Abbey)*

Times have changed since Jane Austen made this cynical observation. Of course inequalities between the sexes still exist, but compared with Jane's experience of life as a woman, we have come a long way and have much to be thankful for.

Jane was a brave, modern, and forward-thinking lady. She was not afraid to defy convention, nor the expectations her social class imposed upon her. She also wrote strong female characters who challenged society's rules and norms. Elizabeth Bennet, in *Pride and Prejudice*, is the prime example of a confident, outspoken, and energetic young woman, very much the opposite of the quiet acquiescence expected of young ladies at that time. With her keen intellect, she is capable of talking about more than just the weather. We see her continually defying convention: she walks miles through muddy fields to visit her sick sister, she turns down an offer of marriage from one of the most eligible bachelors in the country, and then she stands up for herself against the imposing Lady Catherine.

In *Emma*, we are presented with another strong, unmarried heroine. Emma Woodhouse is in an unusual position, as she has become mistress of the household at a young age, her father being unwell. This position, coupled with financial security and her social status, allows her to do as she pleases, without worries for her future, and certainly with no need to marry for security. Women still face challenges today, but at least we can be our own person and speak our mind without fear of judgment.

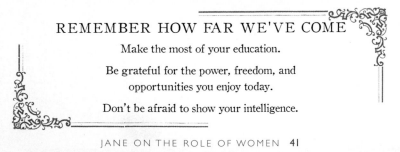

REMEMBER HOW FAR WE'VE COME

Make the most of your education.

Be grateful for the power, freedom, and opportunities you enjoy today.

Don't be afraid to show your intelligence.

MR COLLINS ON THE ART OF FLATTERY
AND ACQUIRING A WIFE

My name is Mr William Collins, cousin of Mr Bennet, and as he has five admirable but, alas, female offspring, I am to inherit his estate upon the unfortunate circumstance of his passing. As Rector of the parish of Hunsford, I believe myself to be exceedingly well regarded by my most esteemed patroness, Lady Catherine de Bourgh. My humble abode abuts her estate, Rosings Park; no doubt the extravagance and magnificence of her house is well known to you by reputation? My noble and wise patroness condescends to favor me with a regular audience, in which to impart her benevolent guidance, and she has recently counseled me to bind myself in the felicitous state of holy matrimony. After my most expeditious and noteworthy success in acquiring an eminently suitable wife, I do believe it is incumbent upon me to instruct those wishing to secure themselves an equally fitting and happy match.

• First, it is of course desirable to secure the eldest daughter of a gentleman of standing. While I myself am to inherit, should one not be in that same happy situation, it is prudent and preferable for one to identify an eldest daughter in a family of moderate wealth. She is likely to bring the larger dowry. I followed this course myself, when first I directed my attentions to my cousin's eldest daughter, Miss Jane Bennet; however, as I was discreetly informed that she was soon to be engaged elsewhere, I immediately lowered my sights to address my interest toward the next in line, Miss Elizabeth Bennet. Having reminded myself of this very point of advice I hereby share, and despite the disappointment Miss Elizabeth must undoubtedly have felt, I am thankful to say that I decided to look elsewhere. My eye soon fell upon my dear Charlotte, who is indeed the eldest daughter in her family. I flatter myself that she welcomed my proposal with appropriate gratitude.

• Next, I recommend one should amuse oneself with arranging such little elegant compliments as may be acceptable to ladies, and bring these into conversation at every opportunity, as this cannot but impress and flatter the happy recipient of one's words. I do believe some gentlemen, more so than others, possess the talent of flattering with delicacy, which is always most pleasing to ladies. I, myself, am blessed with such a gift. Such pleasing attentions will mostly arise from what is passing at the time, although even I will still take time to study and arrange such compliments as may be adapted to ordinary situations. To practice such phrases aloud is a wise course; however, I will advise that it is best to give them as unstudied an air as possible in their delivery.

• My next proposal for attracting one's chosen lady is to read aloud to her, such that she is both entertained and soothed by the mellifluous tone of one's voice. Might I beg to recommend Fordyce's *Sermons to Young Ladies* as a most excellent choice? It relates the most useful lessons on decorous and dignified behavior. Such conduct is becoming in young ladies of a certain standing, especially the lady one views as a prospective partner in matrimony, and a future mistress of one's household.

One should amuse oneself with arranging such little elegant compliments as may be acceptable to ladies, and bring these into conversation at every opportunity.

• One should not be discouraged by any refusal of one's first proposal of marriage. Indeed, it is usual that a young lady should reject the addresses of a man whom she secretly means to accept, when he first applies for her favor, and even that sometimes a refusal should be repeated a second or even a third time. You must understand that the lady seeks further to encourage one's suit by such rebuttal, as is consistent with the true delicacy of the female character. Might I also impress upon you the utmost importance, during a proposal, of pointing out any circumstance which highlights the necessity of the match and, of course, any advantages to the lady of the betrothal. For example, one such encouragement might be a delicate reminder of the age of one's intended, should she be older than one-and-twenty, and therefore unlikely to receive an alternative or more advantageous offer.

I trust that the sagacity of my advice will guide many to secure their desired match, as did I, with my dearest Charlotte. It is the pinnacle of my satisfaction to declare that my patroness thoroughly approves my recent acquirement, so I really could not be more content. I verily believe that my dear Charlotte and I were surely made for one another!

Jane on Simple Pleasures

"I wish as well as everybody else to be perfectly happy;
but, like everybody else it must be in my own way."

(Sense and Sensibility)

In times of solitude, hardship, or even boredom, Austen's characters sometimes escape to their preferred activities: music and playing the piano is a haven for both Marianne Dashwood and Mary Bennet, while Elinor Dashwood favors art and drawing, Captain Benwick loves to study poetry, and Catherine Morland loses herself in a gripping Gothic novel. For Mrs Austen, Jane's mother, gardening was a pleasure that she could enjoy when living in their small cottage, in the village of Chawton.

Doing what makes you happy is essential; we can all benefit from retreating to a favorite place or distracting ourselves from everyday reality with hobbies, interests, and leisure activities; for me, that favorite place is the world of Jane Austen. We know that Jane considered writing as her escape, preferring to "let other pens dwell on guilt and misery." The early 19th-century world was a difficult, turbulent, and often threatening place, and tough things were happening in Jane's own life, in society, and in the wider world, yet she never depicts or refers directly to any actual events of her life and times, thus taking the reader with her into her happier place.

We too live in a difficult world and modern life can be challenging. Remember to make time for what brings *you* pleasure and enjoyment.

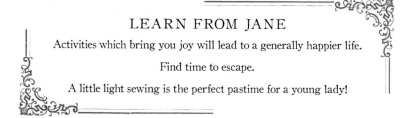

LEARN FROM JANE

Activities which bring you joy will lead to a generally happier life.

Find time to escape.

A little light sewing is the perfect pastime for a young lady!

MISS EMMA WOODHOUSE'S TIPS FOR ORGANIZING A BALL

It is said that to be fond of dancing is a certain step toward falling in love, and as it is every young lady's dream to fall in love, it almost goes without saying that it is essential to attend dances. If you are fortunate enough to live in a fashionable town such as Bath or London, public balls will be commonplace, but if you live in the countryside, in a quiet village similar to Highbury, there are fewer opportunities for dancing. I therefore recommend that you undertake to organize such evenings yourself. Since the success of a recent ball suggested by Mr Frank Churchill, I have taken it upon myself to host such pleasant social evenings frequently, and I now consider myself quite the expert. Here I share with you my thoughts on the correct way to arrange a successful occasion of your own. If you follow my advice, I am certain you will host an impressive and memorable party, and your guests will be begging you to hold another ball before long!

I do recommend you accept offers of help.

• Planning a ball is somewhat more exacting and complicated than you might suspect. I can now understand why my dear friend Mr Weston invited several people to come early on the night of our first ball, to assist with final preparations! I do recommend you accept offers of help, as there are so many things to be arranged, yet you must always give your instructions carefully and keep a watchful eye over the entire occasion.

• I have found that it is preferable to select your invited guests with care, sending invitations only to friends whose company you most enjoy and avoiding any who may cause upset. (I do recall that the Eltons created considerable consternation at our ball, and everyone would much rather they had not been present.)

• It is usual to dispatch invitations a goodly while before the proposed date; this allows your guests to enjoy the excitement of anticipation. However, it might sometimes be better for balls to be held as soon as may be, to avoid the occurrence of any dilemma or predicament that could interrupt your evening, which I have regrettably experienced myself.

• Invite as many gentlemen as you can. It always happens that there will be more beautiful ladies eager to dance than there are handsome and eligible young men to partner them—or, in fact, men of any age! If you have a militia stationed nearby, perhaps you could extend an invitation to their regiment. Officers always make popular dance partners for young ladies!

• Make sure you choose a suitable ballroom; it must be centrally situated, splendidly comfortable, and large enough for a goodly number of dancers, plus the musicians, of course. It is not pleasant to be very overcrowded when dancing!

Invite as many gentlemen as you can.

• Do decorate the ballroom. It is surprising but true that just a very few small embellishments can lift the appearance of a ballroom. Your efforts to make the occasion special are sure to be noticed and commented on by the guests! I do recall the very moment when I first stepped into our ballroom and observed the simple adornments Mr Weston had chosen; they really made the atmosphere of the room quite entrancing! Might I recommend the use of some greenery, such as ivy, to form garlands, with the addition of a few flowers for color?

• Provide a generous and varied selection of dishes for your guests to consume. You would not wish for anyone to go away famished or, worse still, for any frugality of the refreshment to attract negative comment. Indeed, I find guests enjoy themselves all the more when they have eaten well. For quenching the thirst of eager dancers, I highly recommend that a plentiful supply of sweet and spicy Negus be served during the evening, which will also contribute to the merry atmosphere!

• It is essential to employ the services of a competent, well-rehearsed group of musicians, and to instruct them to include a mixture of the slower, more sedate dances with a good number of the delightful and fast-paced country jigs. Every guest will then be able to enjoy their own favorite style of dance!

Jane on Integrity

> "We have all a better guide in ourselves, if we would attend
> to it, than any other person can be."

(Mansfield Park)

Every day, people seek to advise or influence us in our decisions, whether they are small matters or significant ones. Teachers direct our choice of subjects or career; friends suggest what clothes to wear or what music to listen to, parents may try to tell us whether we are dating the right person. And with 21st-century technology, clever marketing constantly tries to influence our spending, while Instagram creates an unrealistic picture of how we should all look.

Often in Austen's novels, when characters allow themselves to be influenced in making a decision, it does not end well. While good advice is always welcome, Jane Austen warns us not to be unduly swayed by the opinions of others, especially when they may have their own motives for interfering.

Emma Woodhouse is driven by her desire to play the matchmaker, and does not take into account Harriet Smith's feelings, or her social status. Poor Harriet is persuaded into believing herself in love with three different men before eventually realizing the one she truly loves is Mr Robert Martin, whom she had fallen for in the first place without encouragement or interference from Emma.

Lady Russell, in *Persuasion*, sincerely believed she was doing her duty and knew what was best for Anne Elliot, when she advised her to break off her original engagement to Captain Wentworth, because of his lack of status and money.

Mr Bingley and Jane Bennet both suffer from the interference of Bingley's sisters and Darcy, who drag Bingley away from Jane and back to London. Mr Darcy has misjudged the strength of Jane's true feelings for Bingley and is later willing to admit his mistake, but Bingley's arrogant sisters are acting in their own interests, not wishing to be related by marriage to a family they see as socially inferior. By allowing himself to be swayed by others, instead of trusting in his own instincts, Bingley almost loses his chance of happiness.

Rather than depending wholly on the advice of others, however well-intentioned it may be, we should learn to make our own decisions. And of course, the reverse is also true—we must be careful when counseling others.

LEARN FROM JANE

Advice can be good, but if it doesn't feel right for you, then make up your own mind.

Only you truly know what is right for you.

Don't expect to sail through smooth waters all your days.

Jane on Family

> "Nobody, who has not been in the interior of a family, can say what the difficulties of any individual of that family may be."

(Emma)

We all know how individuals within families can be vastly different in everything from looks, temperament, and personality, to style, interests, and opinions, yet despite occasional difficulties, family bonds are strong. Of the many families portrayed in Jane Austen's novels, we become particularly well acquainted with the Bennets, the Dashwoods, the Elliots, and the Bertrams.

It goes without saying that we have all had trying times or upsetting experiences when strong family support has proved vital. But as always, Austen gives us a balanced view of family life. As well as illustrating successful families in her novels, she portrays the suffering that comes either because of poor family relations or by missing out on family love altogether.

Fanny Price in *Mansfield Park* is taken away from her parents' home, so that "they are relieved from the charge and expense of one child," and sent to live with her much wealthier cousins, the Bertrams. Unfortunately for her, they do not let her forget that she is the poor relation. Fanny greatly misses her siblings and in particular her brother, William, and she experiences considerable loneliness, despite the attempts of her cousin, Edmund Bertram, to make her feel more welcome.

In *Emma* we see two more examples of children being sent away—Frank Churchill was taken in by wealthy relatives after his mother's death, while Miss Bates was too poor to give a home to Jane Fairfax, her orphaned niece. The importance of family is highlighted in the relationship between aunt and niece: the pride and delight experienced by Miss Bates each time she receives a letter from Jane are so considerable, that she cannot help but share it—endlessly and in minute detail—which tests her friends' patience somewhat!

Jane Austen is clearly writing from experience here. Two of her own brothers left the parental home as children: George, who had health problems, and Edward, who was adopted by the Knight family, rich but childless cousins. Family bonds remained strong, however, and it was eventually thanks to Edward that Jane, Cassandra, and their mother had a place to live in later years. Similarly, in her novel *Sense and Sensibility*, it is a distant relative of the recently widowed Mrs Dashwood who comes to the rescue of the Dashwood family, by providing them with a home for a very low rent. And we know from her letters, particularly to her niece Fanny, that Jane Austen herself was a loving aunt.

It is interesting to notice that even in the more dysfunctional families Austen describes, the heroines are protective of their relations, despite being caused considerable embarrassment by them. Think of Lizzy, standing up for the Bennets in the face of severe criticism from both Darcy and later Lady Catherine de Bourgh. In defending herself against her ladyship's accusations of inferior status, Lizzy defiantly states:

> "He is a gentleman; I am a gentleman's daughter; so far we are equal."

It is clear that the family closeness Jane Austen knew herself is reflected in her stories. Family—whether siblings, parents, cousins, nieces, nephews, aunts, grandfathers—is important, and its bonds should be appreciated and preserved.

LEARN FROM JANE

Treasure the love and support of your family.

You can't choose your family, but you can choose to be proud of them.

Be understanding of each family member and their eccentricities!

MR WOODHOUSE ON HOW TO KEEP SAFE
AND IN GOOD HEALTH

• Life is full of worry; calamities are prone to arise at any moment. One must take precautions and do everything that is sensible to ensure the safety and good health of oneself and others. Above all, do not encourage disaster through careless behavior. I have the extreme good fortune to be in the care of our excellent Mr Perry, who has instructed me on the best path to safety and health. (There is no apothecary so knowledgeable as Mr Perry, you know, nor so reliable and attentive.) Pay close attention to my words of advice below, so that you too will avoid unnecessary perils and unpleasantness.

• Avoid change. An event which engenders any alteration to one's daily routine or displaces loved ones from the family home, such as matrimony, will only cause worriment and dilemma. It is sensible to leave matters as they are. Change brings vexations.

• Do not indulge in cake. Cake is ruinous to one's health—Mr Perry assures me of this fact himself. It is especially injurious to infants and causes them to become exceedingly excitable. But do eat gruel. I always recommend a little gruel before bed. It is so nutritious!

• Walking is such a healthy exercise, that I do propose a daily constitutional. However, you must never walk alone, and I do urge that you avoid roads where gypsies may be present. My daughter Emma's young friend experienced a most unpleasant encounter of this nature. Indeed, it was most shocking! I would counsel your daily walk be taken around your own nice safe garden.

• Young ladies, I must exhort you always to carry a shawl with you for warmth, for even in clement weather you may catch a chill. On one occasion, my dear Emma painted a portrait of her young friend Harriet without a shawl about her shoulders! I was quick to advise her to paint one in.

• It is always preferable to stay at home. If you must travel out of some unavoidable necessity, be sure to allow plenty of time for the journey, and leave early in the day, so that you will not be required to complete your journey in the dark, which is most dangerous. I must also caution you to avoid outings on horseback; rather, you should take a carriage, as this will be far more to your comfort and a considerably safer means for you to undertake your journey. Mr Perry also imparted to me a very clever thing for the winter: if you must venture out at such a dreadful time of year, you must certainly line your carriage with sheepskin!

Life is full of worry; calamities are prone to arise at any moment.

• Do not even contemplate a journey to the seaside, for the air is much purer here in the countryside. But, if you must go, then be sure to visit Cromer rather than Southend, as Mr Perry has assured me it is much healthier in Cromer. Nevertheless, it would be best not to go at all.

• As I have mentioned, all travel is ill-advised, but picnics in the countryside are the most alarming of all outings. It is hardly safe to sit out of doors, and I must impress upon you never even to contemplate eating outdoors— the hazards are too many to consider.

• Be careful of drafts of air, especially if you are to attend a ball. I have heard of young people being so remarkably reprehensible as to open a window, being desirous of fresh air, and what perilous breezes this must create! It is particularly inadvisable when dancing; assembly rooms and such places are already such drafty venues, without more unwelcome currents of air proceeding from an opened window.

• If it is raining, I implore you to stay indoors. Especially you young ladies, who are such delicate creatures. I was once most horrified to learn that our neighbor, Miss Jane Fairfax, had walked to collect her letters from the post office during a treacherous shower of rain! I made sure she would not be so reckless again.

• Be careful of disease and infection, and do not contemplate visiting any friend or relative who is afflicted with a cold, or some such sickness. And be sure to keep them away from your house, for even if there is but a single cough or sneeze, an infection might ensue.

I trust you will follow all my words of advice, which are fully endorsed by Mr Perry also, and that they keep you safe from harm and worry.

Jane on False Friends

"There is nothing I would not do for those who are really my friends. I have no notion of loving people by halves."

(Northanger Abbey)

Isabella Thorpe's remark to Catherine Morland sounds touching, but unfortunately her true nature is quite the opposite of her words. Isabella deliberately befriends Catherine only because she mistakenly believes her to be a rich heiress, and thinks this might be of advantage to her. She also manages to fool Catherine's brother, James, into an engagement.

Jane Austen is obviously well acquainted with false friends: those who profess that they care but are only using us for their own gain. In *Pride and Prejudice*, Caroline Bingley pretends a liking for Jane Bennet, who gullibly trusts her protestations of friendship; yet behind the scenes, Caroline is doing everything she can to get her brother, Mr Bingley, away from Jane.

But it is in *Sense and Sensibility* that we meet perhaps the best illustration of insincerity, in the form of Miss Lucy Steele. Suspecting Edward Ferrars's interest in Elinor, she makes poor Elinor her confidante, swears her to secrecy, and repeatedly reminds her that Edward is secretly engaged to her, and cannot therefore have any attachment to Elinor. Far from being a true friend to Elinor, she is playing the part for her own gain.

We will probably all meet at least one person at some point who seems to be a good friend, but later lets us down. Perhaps they drop us when we are no longer useful to them, maybe they turn their attention to someone else, or they no longer have time for us. This loss can be disappointing, but a false friend is unworthy of our energy and emotions.

LEARN FROM JANE

Don't waste your time on false friends.

True friends know and like the real you.

Identify and value your real friends—they will always be there for you.

Jane on Brothers and Sisters

> "Where shall we see a better daughter, or a kinder sister, or a truer friend?"
>
> *(Emma)*

Jane Austen came from a large family, with six brothers as well as her beloved older sister, Cassandra, who was her closest friend and most trusted confidante. When apart, the two sisters would exchange letters daily, recounting events, problems, and thoughts in great detail.

But let's consider the elder two Dashwood sisters in *Sense and Sensibility*: Elinor is all sense, rationality, and caution, while Marianne is all sensibility, passion, and exuberance. They each face trials and setbacks as the story progresses and, at times, neither can understand the feelings or the behavior of the other. Elinor worries about Marianne's openly passionate love for Mr Willoughby, while Marianne scorns Elinor's quiet and secret admiration for Mr Ferrars. However, their sisterly bond remains firm in adversity, and each learns to appreciate the other's qualities.

In *Pride and Prejudice*, having lost both their parents, Mr Darcy is a caring and protective older brother to his sister Georgiana, despite a big difference in age. The older brother spoils his sister, buying her a new piano, but blames himself for not realizing Wickham's intention to elope with Georgiana before it was almost too late.

In our own families, by understanding and appreciating each individual member, we learn to get along. And as a microcosm of society as a whole, family is where we first learn to live alongside others with tolerance and forbearance, respecting our differences.

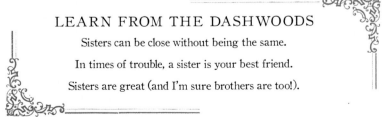

LEARN FROM THE DASHWOODS

Sisters can be close without being the same.

In times of trouble, a sister is your best friend.

Sisters are great (and I'm sure brothers are too!).

Jane on Money

> "A large income is the best recipe for
> happiness I ever heard of."

(Mansfield Park)

Jane Austen makes frequent reference to money and income in both her novels and her letters, but these are often tongue in cheek or humorous comments! Remember the famous first sentence of *Pride and Prejudice*, often voted the greatest opening line in literature:

> "It is a truth universally acknowledged, that a single man in
> possession of a good fortune must be in want of a wife."

Mrs Bennet takes great delight in assessing the single gentlemen of her acquaintance in terms of annual income, particularly as they are all viewed as prospective suitors for her five daughters. Mr Bingley is worth £5,000, but Mr Darcy is worth double that amount! Nevertheless, such observations do, somewhat reluctantly, acknowledge that wealth is a significant fact of life. Lizzy Bennet teases her sister, Jane, by admitting she fell in love with Darcy on "first seeing his beautiful grounds at Pemberley." Jane is soon reassured that Lizzy has said this in jest: "Another entreaty that she would be serious, however, produced the desired effect; and she soon satisfied Jane by her solemn assurances of attachment."

Jane Austen herself enjoyed spending money. On one particularly expensive shopping trip, she had been tempted to buy such fripperies as some pretty muslin, trimmings, and three pairs of silk stockings, and later admitted in a letter to her sister, Cassandra:

> "I am sorry to tell you that I am getting very extravagant,
> and spending all my money, and, what is worse for you,
> I have been spending yours too."

However, Austen equally portrays the hardships which face those struggling financially, through characters such as "poor Miss Bates" in *Emma*, and Anne Elliot's impoverished friend, Mrs Smith, in *Persuasion*.

And importantly, Anne's compassion is contrasted with the snobbery and self-importance of her family, while Emma's thoughtlessness toward Miss Bates is soon reprimanded by Mr Knightley. It seems that while Jane Austen knew the value of money, she also understood the difficulties of those who were less fortunate than others.

Money divides society now, just as it did in the Regency era. We may not be judged in terms of our financial worth to the same extent as Mrs Bennet loves to do, but stark differences in people's disposable income are evident in everyday society. And life without sufficient income is always more challenging.

LEARN FROM JANE

Regrettably, money is a necessity of life.

Wealth comes with responsibilities—be a Mr Darcy, not a Sir Walter Elliot.

Money isn't everything—but it does make life easier!

LIST OF ILLUSTRATIONS

ACKNOWLEDGMENTS

I would like to thank Mrs Shirwani for fueling my initial passion for Jane Austen at school. My sincere appreciation goes to my mother Jane, my sister Charlotte, and my dear friends Hazel, Alinka, Ailsa, and Gabby for their support while I was writing this book. I am incredibly grateful to my inspirational friend Jane Odiwe for the beautiful illustrations and huge thanks to the amazing team at CICO Books for their help and advice. Thank you to all the wonderful Janeite friends I have made in this unique community over the years. And finally, thank you to the Jane Austen Pineapple Appreciation Society for all the love and support that only true friends can give.

And of course, thank you Jane Austen!

INDEX